The Essential Handbook for
First-Time
Managers &
Supervisors

Ten Lessons to Easy Management Success

The Essential Handbook for First-Time Managers & Supervisors

Ten Lessons to Easy Management Success

by **Pam Boyd**

SkillPath Publications

Editor: Bill Cowles

Layout and cover design: Jason Sprenger

ISBN: 978-1-929874-97-2

10 9 8 7 6 5 4   10

Printed in the United States of America

Table of Contents

Foreword

Congratulations or condolences … you're the boss!

This is exciting! You've been promoted to supervisor! Or perhaps you were finally anointed *"Manager,"* even though you've been doing the work of a manager for a long time.

Whatever your circumstance, congratulations! It feels good, doesn't it? At last someone has noticed your exceptional performance and is finally giving you the credit you deserve. Be proud of yourself and take the time to celebrate your achievement, because it is something to celebrate!

The world needs more excellent leadership and you stepped up to the plate. You earned the job and now you have the opportunity to influence more people, to better utilize your leadership skills and to multiply the impact you have upon your organization. Thank you for showing the initiative, the excellence and the work ethic necessary for your promotion!

You have earned our "thanks" because your success impacts all of us. Have you ever heard of the "butterfly effect"? If you haven't seen the movie, the theory suggests that every act, even one as small as the beat of a small butterfly's wings, affects the entire world. It's the theory that we all are connected to one another in some way—that what you do matters, if not directly then indirectly, *to everyone.* In other words, when you succeed, I succeed!

So, let's get on with the show, let's make sure you're headed in the right direction, and let's make sure you have the tools you need to not just survive—but absolutely *thrive*—in this new role!

Pam

Pam Boyd

Lesson 1:
Getting Started

The Reluctant Manager

"What you can do or think you can do; begin it.
For boldness has magic, power and genius in it."

— *Goethe*

This is for those of you who are "reluctant" supervisors. Many of you never intended to be in this role. You were satisfied doing your own job with pride, minding your own business, and you never wanted the headaches of being responsible for someone else's performance.

I can thoroughly relate to your experience. Those were my feelings before being offered my first supervisory position. I was one of those associates who said, "I wouldn't have a management job for a million bucks!" but, subconsciously, always wanted to be considered a viable candidate for the job. And when the offer came, for better or worse, I took the plunge.

How hard could it be, anyway? I had read a few books about dealing with people and knew I could out-manage all of my former bosses. I wanted to show them how to be nice to people and still get the job done! After all, it was simple—treat people right and they'll treat you right. Right?

Boy, did I have a lot to learn. The lessons were painful. My "treat-people-right-and-they'll-treat-you-right plan" didn't work, so I scrambled to find other methods that might produce better results for me. I didn't really have a mentor or know where to turn for help, so I got busy reinventing the wheel. Many times I thought I wasn't going to make it. I questioned my sanity for ever taking the position in the first place and wondered if my life would have been better had I just said "no" to the be-the-boss offer.

But now, after years of learning by trial and error, I am thankful that I took the risk and "the road less traveled." It has made all the difference, and I now have techniques, tools and lessons to pass on so that *you* won't have to learn these lessons the hard way!

The Terrified Manager

> *"No great deed, private or public, has ever been undertaken in a bliss of certainty."*
>
> — *Leon Wieseltier*

For those of you who are more than reluctant, who are sweating this out, afraid you will fail, afraid people will hate you, afraid everyone will think you are a big fraud—rest assured that these feelings of trepidation are totally and completely normal.

Every great leader has had to deal with self-doubt and similar feelings of inadequacy at some time during his or her career. You are not alone. Leading people *is* an ominous task! There will be difficult days. There will be difficult lessons. There will be days when you will stand alone for your principles. There will be days when you will feel totally ineffective, when you will feel like you are accomplishing nothing. But there will also be days when you will see great results, when you will make a vast difference, when you will glow with victory.

Take comfort in the knowledge that today, all over this country and all over the world, conscientious men and women like you are arriving at this crossroad and are deciding to step into this awesome, although sometimes overwhelming, adventure called management.

And if they can do it, so can you!

Lesson 2:
Taking
the Lead

Who's Ready to Lead?

Have you ever worked for a jerk? Most of us have. Since statistics show that 85% of all managers have had no management training, it is not surprising that the majority of us have had the unfortunate experience of working for someone who didn't have a clue about what a real leader would do and, consequently, acted like a jerk!

There is also such an incredible scarcity of leadership in the world that incompetent people sometimes land in the role of manager because there was *no one else available* to do the job! You know this is true. History testifies, in case after case: The human race has been *so desperate* for someone, *anyone*, to be the leader, that we've willingly followed tyrants and dictators who merely disguised themselves as leaders.

In my early management days, I criticized upper management for being oblivious and disinterested in finding good leadership. I reasoned like this: If they were looking, they would have noticed me! But, in reality, upper management *had* noticed me—they'd noticed I wasn't ready—and that's why I was passed over for promotions.

Leaders are in high demand!

Now, after doing my time on the corporate upper-management side, I know that corporate decision-makers are *very interested* in finding good leadership. In fact, the first agenda item in every staff meeting, every week, in every corporate office is probably—"Who's ready to lead?" People in positions of power everywhere are asking this question. Even in your job, you are always trying to find someone who can handle more responsibility, aren't you? The trouble is that mature leadership is rare. So if you want to be the person decision-makers are looking for, it's simple; just do what a leader would do, in every situation in which you find yourself.

Be the Boss You Admire

Many of you have had the privilege of working for someone who set a good leadership example, or you have had a parent or a coach whom you admired. My role models were people whom I read about—Abraham Lincoln, Henry V, Lafayette, Mother Teresa, to mention just a few. Because I didn't really know anyone personally who could serve as my mentor, I read countless biographies of successful leaders in order to glean nuggets of truth and wisdom from their experiences. Here is a quote from Napoleon Bonaparte that has encouraged me along the way. Napoleon summed up leadership in these few words:

> *"A leader is a vendor of hope."*

This quote succinctly describes the primary role of a leader, which is *not* being a baby sitter. If you've ever wondered what that primary role was, here it is: A leader is a salesperson. A leader is selling hope!

You might say, "I'm not in sales. I'm in management." Yes, but if you are managing people, you are asking them to "buy" your agenda. You are attempting to interest others in what you think is important. And that's not an easy task. Trying to motivate the X and Y generations, for instance, brings its own set of challenges, as does working with associates who are close to retirement or who may work for the government or a union.

Great leaders throughout history have also had difficult audiences but, nevertheless, have successfully "sold" the most incredible agendas to their followers. 15th-century England's King Henry V is one of them. The following story illustrates why he is an exemplary "vendor of hope":

Henry had been drawn into war against France, but his army was not quite ready for the terrific challenge the French army brought against England. The English were outnumbered ten to one and were not doing well in battle. Henry's men were cold, tired, hungry and defeated, and reinforcements had not come from England. A major battle was to take place the next morning. Henry walked through the camp and heard his men grumbling, complaining and even despairing. The men knew they were probably going to die. They had already lost some of their best men. Even Henry's cousin and first officer, Westmoreland, had given up hope.

But, instead of becoming negative like everyone else, Henry did what only a leader could do. He chose to take the high road and he remained courageous. He knew if he could get the morale of his soldiers up, they would have a chance of winning. So Henry encouraged his troops by delivering the famous speech of Saint Crispin's.

In that speech, Henry first of all gave anyone who wanted to go back home permission to do so. He said he only wanted those to stay with him who wanted to save and honor England. He told them that whoever stayed and shed their blood with him would be his brothers. He also told his men that *he was glad* reinforcements had not come from England, because if they had, their army would be forced to share the glory with the reinforcements for what they would accomplish in the battle. He reminded them that their names would become household words in England; that good men would tell of their feats to their children and grandchildren; and that every year on Saint Crispin's Day, those who survived the fray would proudly display their battle scars as heroes! He ended the speech by labeling his formerly downtrodden, despairing army with this famous description, " … *we few, we happy few, we band of brothers!*"

As a result of his rousing speech, Henry's men were inspired to go into battle with new resolve. Their spirits were renewed; they had new strength and new hope! And guess what happened? The English Army defeated the French, against ten-to-one odds, sustaining only twenty-five casualties in the process. That's the power of a leader who is a "vendor of hope."

Have you ever had this kind of experience? Have you heard negative talk at your job? Have you been discouraged because you didn't know what to do to improve morale or to stop the downward spiral? This is not an easy situation to handle, and King Henry V must have felt discouraged and frustrated as well.

A leader who is a "vendor of hope" is a leader who knows that people will have hope if they are given the assurance inherent in these two S-words: *Significance* and *security*.

The Two "S" Words: Significance and Security

When a person feels significant and/or secure, that person has hope. King Henry was able to give his men *significance* by reminding them of the things they really wanted: To be brave, to be remembered as heroes, to make a difference, to be connected and associated with honorable men. They wanted to be noble.

Henry offered them the *security* they craved by restoring their confidence in themselves and in each other. Once his men felt secure and significant again, they had hope. Their hope translated into action, and that action led to victory.

Are you ready to lead like this? Are you ready to be a "vendor of hope," assuring your associates of their *significance* and their *security?* Are you ready when you encounter your own obstacles to do only *what a leader would do?* When you are tempted to do what everyone else does, when you are tempted to complain, when you are tempted to lose your positive attitude, will you instead do what a mature leader would do?

Have you pre-programmed your subconscious mind with inspiring stories from your heroes or role models, similar to this one about Henry V? Doing so will transform you into a "vendor of hope"—a leader who assists others by helping them feel *significant* and *secure.*

Most managers do not focus on becoming a real leader because they just don't know where to find the time to do so. They're too busy solving problems, taking care of everyday challenges and simply surviving to find the time to really analyze and develop their role. It is not only *easier* to go with the flow; often it seems like the only option available! But when you take the role of leader seriously and remember your primary responsibility as a "vendor of hope," you will experience a very high level of satisfaction in your career.

This path *is* the "road less traveled," but there is an essential, time-tested plan that will help you find your way down that road.

Lesson 3:
Following the "Essential Plan"

What is the "Essential Plan"?

The "Essential Plan" has been successfully employed by the most powerful leaders of all time.

- **Communicate** clear expectations
- **Reward** performers
- **Coach** for better performance
- **Do not tolerate** poor performers

This plan is not complicated. It's not difficult to remember. It's not tricky. But even though it is amazingly simple and straightforward, the staggering truth is that most managers are not using this method and, consequently, not experiencing the type of results that make supervising a *manageable* experience.

At Work With the Essential Plan

When going on business to Grand Rapids, Michigan, I noticed on my itinerary that I was booked to stay in a chain hotel that I considered mediocre at best. My flight was delayed and when I finally arrived in Grand Rapids it was after midnight. Surprisingly, the shuttle from the hotel was still there waiting for me, the driver was extremely kind and thoughtful, even at that late hour, and when I walked into the hotel, I was stunned by the appearance and cleanliness of the facility. I thought I must have been dropped off at the wrong hotel by mistake! The remainder of my stay there was similarly surprising, down to and including my shuttle ride back to the airport.

When I approached Ben, the teenage clerk at the front desk, to ask for a ride to the airport, he was very helpful and said that the shuttle driver would be available in ten minutes. I busied myself getting my luggage ready and was surprised when, ten minutes later, Ben came bounding over the counter, donning the shuttle-driver jacket. As Ben loaded my bags into the hotel van, he explained that the driver was running late so he was going to honor his commitment by driving me to the airport.

On the way, I complimented Ben on his exceptional commitment to customer service. I told him that in my experience, an employee his age with such an aggressive customer-service stance was a rarity.

I said, "Ben, you've just disproved the theory that your generation doesn't possess the same work ethic as previous generations. So what's with you and the other employees at this hotel, anyway? Why is this hotel so different from the other hotels in the chain?"

Ben stunned me with his reply. I expected him to say he didn't know or that his parents had raised him right, but instead he said, "I'll tell you exactly why this hotel is different. It's because the general manager of this hotel sets an incredible example of what customer service means. He does whatever is necessary to communicate genuine concern for our guests and he also makes it perfectly clear that he expects that same level of commitment from everyone who works here."

"How does he do that? How does he make it perfectly clear?" I asked.

"Well, if you do what he asks, you get rewarded."

"Do you mean you get raises?"

"Sometimes, but that's not what I mean," Ben said. "He does other things for you."

"Like what?" I asked.

"We have all kinds of incentives, little things like movie tickets, contests, and other incentives that aren't so little. For example, I just started college and when I told my boss I was interested in Hospitality Management, he paid for my books."

"Wow. That's nice."

"Yeah, but then, on the other hand, if you don't perform, you don't last long."

"Do you mean he just fires you? This hotel must have a lot of turnover."

"No, not at all. Like I said, you know what you're getting into right from the start. The training is thorough and if you mess up, you know about it immediately. And if you're improving, the manager works with you. But there's no tolerance for people who don't care. Best job I've ever had!"

When Ben finished talking, it was clear that his description of his manager's approach was a perfect example of the Essential Plan. Did you notice the elements?

- **Communicate clear expectations**—the manager communicated exactly what he wanted through words and actions

- **Reward performers**—the manager was creative and had multiple ways to reward performers

- **Coach for better performance**—the manager worked one-on-one with anyone who made the effort to improve

- **Do not tolerate poor performance**—the manager set high standards and was quick to take action to maintain those standards

Sounds easy, doesn't it? Again, it's simple … but it's not easy! If it were easy, every manager would be using this method and obviously they're not. So let's look into each element more thoroughly.

Lesson 4:
Communicating
Clear
Expectations

Do I Have to Be a Cheerleader?

At a management seminar in New Hampshire, a participant said: "I'm the director of nursing in a large hospital and I really like my job, but because I'm not outgoing and I don't really smile much, frequently my employees complain about me to the administrator. They say I make them feel insecure and they think I'm angry with them when that's not the case."

I suggested to him, "Since a smile is a signal, a kind of welcome mat that helps others judge your approachability, smiling is an essential management tool. If you don't have a smile you must compensate for its lack with words of assurance."

He then said, "But, I don't like to talk either."

"Well," I said, "I hope you're pinning notes to your lab coat, because somehow, somewhere along the way, your associates need to know what you're thinking! You're their leader. How do they know where you're going?"

His response was typical of a lot of us: "I set a good example. Isn't that enough? It seems to me that they need to adjust to *me*. Why do I have to adjust to them?"

Good question! Not all of us are dynamic, extroverted, polished public speakers. So does it matter if we don't like to talk much? Do we all have to be cheerleaders?

Of course not. There's room for every personality style in the management ranks. One can find excellent examples of leadership among introverts as well as extroverts. But plenty of evidence does exist to support the correlation between good speaking and good results. Even Quintilian, the father of modern education, emphasized this correlation. He said, "The object of education is to produce good men who speak well. If a man speaks well but is not good, he will be a tyrant. But if he is good, but does not speak well, his influence and impact will be limited."

Join the "FCC"—Frequent Communicators Club

The psychological impact of the lack of verbal communication is profound! Studies have shown that the more communication we receive as children, the more confident we will be as adults. Even when we are no longer children, we still need affirmation and approval, direction and redirection. Good leaders know this. Good leaders constantly work to improve their communication skills. Good leaders know the power of consistent communication.

So even if you're not a chatterbox or a cheerleader, it is of paramount importance that you belong to the FCC (Frequent Communicators Club). If you want people to be on the same page with you, you have to "show them the page" in as many ways as you can think of. If they are on the same page with you it won't be an accident. It will because you were aware that showing them the page was your number one priority!

How can I get more out of every minute?

In a class called Maximizing Your Leadership Potential, the content was simple—we merely dissected the average day of the attendee and broke it down into very small segments. We asked these two questions: "How could this segment be better utilized?" and "What would a leader do in this circumstance?" Very frequently the answer to each of these questions was, "I could use this segment of my day to share information more often and more thoroughly."

In our hotel manager example, Ben said that he knew clearly what he was getting into before he started the job. We must assume that during the interview process the manager:

- Explained his vision and his passion for customer service

- Determined that Ben could grasp his vision

- Assessed Ben's willingness and ability to display similar passion for customer service

- Explained practical elements of the customer service job to Ben

Ben also mentioned that once he was hired, the manager:

- Set a clear and consistent example of exceptional customer service

- Continued to communicate clear expectations

Discover the Power of Under-utilized Tools

Communicating clear expectations is not a one-time thing; it's an ongoing management duty that never ceases. The opportunities to pass on clear expectations are virtually unlimited. Following are some under-utilized tools that Ben's manager probably used to clarify and reinforce performance expectations.

Job description

Frequently, managers look at job descriptions as needless documents that should be labeled "Refer to only in case of legal dispute." If you have a similar ambivalence toward them, realize that a good job description is a remarkable tool you can use to keep associates on the same page. If the document is actually a *thorough and practical description* of a job, it can not only keep you out of legal hot water but will also be functional for hiring, counseling, performance reviews, giving raises or rewards, cross-training and firing. Of course, the problem is that most job descriptions are not. They are too vague, too general, too outdated and too buried in the files to be useful!

To improve the usefulness of your job descriptions, ask yourself these questions:

1. If I had to terminate someone right now for a performance issue, are the missing performance criteria explicit in the job description?

2. If I began the disciplinary process with an associate for a lack of teamwork, for instance, are there enough tangible and exact specifications in their job description to illustrate teamwork expectations—e.g., answer the phone before it rings three times, greet a customer within five seconds of arrival, keep windows fingerprint-free, etc.?

3. Would the job description be completely functional as a performance appraisal document?

Associate handbook

An associate handbook is only as functional as it is reflective of the passion and vision of the leaders of the company. Does yours reflect the mission statement of the organization without boring people to tears? Is it concise enough to be useful but detailed enough to answer operational questions? If not, it will only sit on the shelf and gather dust. And to the extent a manager uses the handbook in meetings, coaching, hiring, etc., the associates will refer to the essential information in the book to that same extent. (You may even want to hide some answers to bonus questions within the text of the book and give out small prizes at associate meetings to those who find the answers. This will get them reading the handbook.)

What a shame to spend all the time and effort producing such a book and use it so little! No one really likes spending the time necessary to write or update manuals, but it's one of those things that will pay off nicely in the long run. Invest now in a tool that will give you leverage—or struggle through problems as they steal your time and morale away, bit by bit. You will either pay now or pay later!

Orientation

> *"When you do the common things in life in an uncommon way,*
> *you will command the attention of the world!"*
>
> — *George Washington Carver*

Have you ever started a job where your boss just "threw you in and hoped you would eventually figure things out"? Was it fun? No. Most likely, you were riddled with anxiety. In fact, most new employees fail not because they don't have the capability to do the work but because they were not given a good start, were not given enough direction and were consequently sabotaged by their fear of failure!

Fear is a thief of competence. Your job as a manager is to remove that fear before it ever has the chance to rear its ugly head. Orientation is the perfect opportunity to use your management leverage right from the beginning; to infect associates with your passion, your mission, your vision. Unfortunately, most managers do not cash in on this wonderful opportunity.

As a result, the average orientation is pathetically mediocre, boring and perfunctory. And which is worse—providing no orientation at all or forcing someone to sit through a boring, uninspired orientation? Please, please, please do not add any more *boring* to the world! We've all had way too much of that in our lives already.

Instead, start an associate out with a powerful connection to your organization. This is your big chance to make a lasting first impression and set the associate up for success. In the orientation, bring a passionate and genuine commitment to their personal development plan. Tell about the learning curve and what mistakes to expect. Help the associate feel your investment in their success!

Training materials

"Enthusiasm finds the opportunities, and energy makes the most of them."

— Henry Hoskins

Besides traditional business materials, smart managers will also reference mainstream movies, music, TV programs and even computer games to teach and reinforce valuable principles. Speak to your associates where they live, through their culture, in their "language."

Jan, an associate in the restaurant business, was getting burned out after twenty-plus years of managing in the field. But then her manager suggested she try a new computer game he'd found which was based on the restaurant business. The object of the game was to get faster and more efficient in caring for restaurant patrons. The faster and more efficient players became, the more points they accumulated and, consequently, the more leverage they earned to grow and improve "the business." Sounds like real business, doesn't it? Yes, but it's a game and it's fun! So, ironically, after working a twelve- or fourteen-hour day, Jan frequently played this game at home, sometimes until two or three in the morning.

It sounds crazy, but the game re-ignited Jan's waning enthusiasm for the business of taking care of restaurant patrons. When she remembers the game and scores herself at work, she experiences even more satisfaction in her work. She also utilizes the game's concept of points for speed and efficiency of service to create a fun contest for her staff.

Training doesn't have to be boring.

Employee meetings

Unfortunately, prior experience has programmed us to expect very little from meetings. All of us have listened to so many boring teachers, preachers and bosses in our lifetimes that when we hear the "M" word, we automatically think "boring" or "waste of time," don't we?

> *If you are boring people, you are stealing from them. You are stealing their time, their energy and possibly their happiness!*

So, besides using the creative means previously discussed, what else can you do to ensure your meetings are not boring but are instead engaging and interesting?

The most important thing you can do is to use the number one rule of the sales industry: *Address the needs of your listeners!*

You have no audience unless you're talking about what your audience wants. They may be in the room with you, but they're not listening. They are thinking about how much longer you're going to talk, their to-do list or what's for dinner.

So before you plan your meeting, ask yourself, "What do my associates want?" After you figure out the answer to that question, frame every agenda item around that one thing. If they want fun, give them games, skits or movie clips at your meeting. If they want money, tell them how to get on the path to make more money and give a $5 or $10 prize at the meeting to someone who is setting a good example. If they want fewer meetings, tell them what they have to do to have fewer meetings.

The second most important thing you can do is to *speak with passion and speak from your heart!* Have you ever been in a meeting that was taken over by a "drama and trauma queen (or king)" and it turned into a gripe session? That can happen to you too, if you're not leading your meeting with passion. And if you're uncomfortable with public speaking, *being passionate about your topic* is one of the best remedies for this debilitating fear. Don't think about your audience; think about how badly your audience *needs to hear what you have to say.* Think about how important your message is and how your message will impact the lives and careers of your associates. When you're focused on your mission, your focus on yourself and your fears will diminish.

The keys to a successful meeting? Try these techniques:

- Start your meeting with an inspiring quote or story about the power of teamwork. Real stories connect with the heart! If you don't have one, find one in a book or on an audio CD, or look one up on the Web. You can even go to www.npr.org. There's a story there on just about any topic you need!

- Practice your tone and volume before the meeting. Speaking with authority involves speaking louder and more deliberately and demonstrates confidence to your associates. Let them know that you're comfortable being in charge.

- Assign portions of the meeting to associates who have set good examples of the work habits you desire. Ask them to relate their experiences and help their peers mirror their behavior.

- Use a skit or a comedy routine. Comedy is the medium of the day. And you probably have at least one associate (if it isn't you) who is a royal comedian: Get a couple of your funny people together and prepare skits for your meetings. This will change things! Once, when I was having difficulty with too much gossiping and back-stabbing at work, I asked our "drama and trauma queen" to put a skit together about the subject. She did and it was so funny that the associates weren't even upset when I told them that gossip would no longer be tolerated on the premises and would, henceforth, be considered grounds for termination.

If you need further help with making your meetings better, you may want to take the "Bore Score" test included in the Appendix. But whatever you do, *stop delivering boring meetings!*

Mentoring

Mentoring is probably the most under-utilized of all the tools available to you. "Mentoring" is not the common practice of having a designated "trainer" in your workplace—effective mentoring is much more comprehensive than that. I'm referring to a practice that involves the thoughtful pairing of individuals who will complement each other's knowledge base and, consequently, the knowledge base *and morale* of the entire team. Effective mentoring will help you communicate clear expectations, associate to associate. Here are some examples of effective mentoring pairs that successful companies use:

- **High-tech Associate/Reluctant-to-Use-Technology Associate**—This pairing will stop frustration on both sides. The low-tech associate often feels very insecure around members of the X or Y generation who are at ease with technology. On the other hand, younger people are tempted to be critical and frustrated with older generations who refuse to "come into the 21st century." By forcing the dependency (and potential friendship) of pairs of this type, you make it less embarrassing for low-techies to ask for help and you'll give high-tech associates the opportunity to gain credibility with associates who may have been around longer. This pairing is particularly important when your workplace is transitioning to a new system or initiating technology upgrades.

One manager used this mentoring relationship to ease the pain of a major technology upgrade in a government office. After assigning the mentoring pairs, she initiated a contest for the team who was the most positive and proactive about the change. As a result, the morale of her department, which was normally very low during system changes, skyrocketed!

- **Corporate Associate/Field Associate**—This is sometimes referred to as the "office buddy" system and is very effective when there is a lack of trust on either side. Field people tend to think the office personnel have it easy and don't really have a clue about the work that occurs "on the front lines." Office personnel tend to think the field associates are "cry babies" and unnecessarily demanding. By assigning an "office buddy" to a field associate, you are giving formerly judgmental associates an opportunity to understand and identify with the demands of the "other side."

- **New Associate/Close-to-Retirement Associate**—This relationship can work miracles in restoring waning interest in the job by someone who is ready to retire. The enthusiasm of the new associate can be infectious. And the benefit of tested knowledge from the tenured associate is priceless for the new associate.

- **Peer Counterparts**—This mentoring relationship is crucial if you are dealing with distrust and jealousy involving multiple locations for the same business. Healthy competition is great, but if there is no camaraderie between sites, why not pair associates with their counterparts in another location. This works great for sharing knowledge and saving time and money that would be invested reinventing the wheel.

When you put some time and thought into this technique of setting up mentoring relationships, you will multiply your power and bring hope and freshness to your organization. The manager's primary role in facilitating the effectiveness of these relationships is to make sure they remain a priority. A manager must provide opportunities for social interaction for the mentor teams and must reward those who use the tool.

These are by no means the only avenues available for you to communicate clear expectations to your staff. But these are the most neglected avenues. Your opportunities are virtually unlimited, but you will miss many opportunities unless you remind yourself that communicating clear expectations is the pathway to *getting the results you need!*

It's so easy to assume associates know what you want when they really don't. Here's a checklist that will help ensure that you have set clear expectations:

✔ Setting Clear Expectations Checklist

1. Do you thoroughly understand what's expected of you?   [Yes] [No]

2. Are you crystal clear about how to measure your own success or how your boss is measuring your success?   [Yes] [No]

3. If your associates meet the expectations that you have set for them, will that give you the results you need?   [Yes] [No]

4. Do you have a mission/vision statement?   [Yes] [No]

5. Do your associates' job descriptions accurately reflect the requirements of the job?   [Yes] [No]

6. Do you have a concise way of explaining these expectations in a job interview?   [Yes] [No]

7. Are new-hire orientations a top priority?   [Yes] [No]

8. Do you use an associate handbook?   [Yes] [No]

9. Are you using current cultural references to teach valuable principles to your associates?   [Yes] [No]

10. Do associates look forward to your meetings?   [Yes] [No]

11. Do you encourage a team or mentoring approach to achieving company goals?   [Yes] [No]

12. Are you passionate about your expectations?   [Yes] [No]

If you answered "no" to any of these questions, you may not be communicating clear expectations. Crucial information may be falling through the cracks.

Use this checklist on a regular basis to find out where the problems are and to remind yourself to focus on keeping everyone on the same page. Then, when everyone *is* on the same page, *keep them there* by following the next step of the Essential Plan.

Lesson 5:
Rewarding Performers

What Do Your Associates Want?

We learned from Pavlov's experiments with dogs that there's great power in positive reinforcement to elicit specific behaviors. Many of you are very good at using rewards with your associates already. This isn't rocket science. The dynamic is simple—your associates will give you the behavior that brings them the best rewards! Problems occur when we don't understand what our associates want or when we have no way of rewarding our performers; e.g., there is a raise freeze, our associates work for a union that limits our ability to reward them or our boss holds tight reins on the checkbook. Sometimes the problem is that the associates are getting better rewards for *not doing what we ask them to do.*

CASE IN POINT

A company that operates restaurants requested help dealing with a serious theft problem in one of their out-of-state locations. The location was difficult to staff, so they had invested a lot of money locating and training managers in that town. Unfortunately, *every* manager they had employed had demonstrated poor inventory control and consistently high operating costs.

Analysis determined that the relatively small community surrounding the location was very close-knit. The business was a popular hangout, the managers were well known around town, and the managers earned clout in the community if they "hooked up" their friends by giving away free food and drink. The managers were not earning bonuses by meeting the corporate cost-control targets, but they were getting bonuses from other sources. For their generosity with their employer's goods, the managers were enjoying high esteem in the community and were receiving under-the-table benefits from other businesses. To sum up, the pay-off *for not meeting their company's cost objectives* was better than the pay-off for meeting the objectives.

In order for the company to turn this situation around, they had to set up a program that would give the managers an incentive to be honest that was greater than the incentive they had to be dishonest. Upper management not only had to inspect and enforce the rules; they also had to make keeping the rules rewarding. But in order to provide alluring rewards, the company had to *know* what would be a highly sought-after incentive.

An important question

To discover what rewards work, you must know what people want. To get insightful information about this, you must ask them what they want in a creative manner. Otherwise, you're just going to hear "Money!" in response to your question. Try asking the question like this: "If I needed better performance from you, but couldn't give you a raise or a bonus to reward you for the additional work, what else could I give you?" You may be surprised at the varied responses you will hear to this question.

The company I just referred to discovered that their managers wanted community recognition and *free stuff*. So they set up a program with the chamber of commerce to acknowledge their integrity and cost controls. The manager who met financial targets was honored with a front page story in the newspaper, with an awards ceremony and with a vacation package. That got their attention and costs came back in line.

A seminar participant said that he used this question with his associates and got an unusual answer. He worked in a high-tech company that employed primarily men and women in the "Y generation." The number one answer to the question was, "Give us a paintball tournament!" From another manager I heard this response: "The majority of my associates are close to retirement. The number one answer was, 'We would like a grandparent's day so that we can bring our grandkids to work and show them off.'" Interesting!

Many times, though, the answer to this question is simply: Recognize me. Notice me. Tell me how much it mattered that I went the extra mile. Tell me how I made a difference. Tell me how much you appreciated my effort, because that *makes me feel significant!* When people feel significant they perform at a higher level.

In one of my first jobs as a waitress, I worked in a high-volume restaurant that had very low morale. The kitchen staff worked in a cramped and unbearably hot kitchen, but kept up with an incredible number of orders. They did the work, but their negative attitudes affected the entire mood of the restaurant. I had read some books about management and saw the problem immediately: The cooks needed to be recognized for their efforts, especially considering the difficult conditions in which they worked. Being the young know-it-all that I was, I took matters into my own hands and immediately cornered the manager.

"Mr. Gonzales, did you know that the cooks are not very motivated in the kitchen? If you could give them some positive reinforcement, the morale in this place would really improve!" I spouted, believing I was about to get a gold star for my brilliant idea. Instead, Mr. Gonzales barely looked at me and dismissed my enthusiasm with, "They get their paychecks."

They get their paychecks? That was his idea of positive reinforcement? I was stunned! But, if I had been more worldly wise I might have anticipated this response and would have known that many managers function according to that same philosophy; the paycheck is sufficient reward for work performed.

The Downside to Giving Recognition

Most of us have worked for bosses like Mr. Gonzales. And most of us know that *getting a paycheck is not enough*. We know that we need more than a paycheck to feel valuable at work. We need recognition. We also know that the most difficult days in our own career have been those days when we felt as if no one was noticing our hard work. We know that a little acknowledgment goes a long way when it comes to helping our morale. We've seen the magic that this one tool can work. But most managers don't use this management tool enough. Why? Because giving recognition has a definite downside.

"So where's my raise?"

Sometimes when you give recognition for a job well done, the recipient of your praise will get a big fat head and look you straight in the eye and say, "So where's my raise?" And, then you squirm and stutter and have no options but to put them off or simply turn down their request. Consequently, both of you feel bad and the recognition will serve *only* to de-motivate. You get discouraged and decide next time you're going to just keep your mouth shut.

So what do you do about this situation? How do you recognize performers without experiencing negative repercussions?

In this situation, it's important to not get intimidated. With confidence you can respond, "I'm not able to give you a raise at this time, but I can assure you that by continuing the behavior that warranted this recognition and by meeting your performance expectations, you have set yourself on a path of professional growth with this company. If you respond maturely without a raise now, people will notice. There are other ways this company rewards performers and I will be your advocate to make sure that you're receiving what you deserve."

"Yeah, well, what about me?"

And here's another situation: You've been told to correct in private and praise in public, but when you do make praise a public affair, there are the jealous employees who play the political card against you without fail. These associates immediately spread rumors that the recipient of the praise is "teacher's pet," the recipient has something going on the side, the manager is blind to the truth about the recipient and so on. This whole dynamic makes recognizing people a royal pain in the you-know-what.

Jealousy!

Don't we all know about this one! When someone receives recognition, and that someone is not them, jealous associates seethe, criticize, pout and plant seeds of discontent with the other associates. For them, recognition programs become a *de-motivator* because they feel that they are being excluded unfairly.

CASE IN POINT

During my early management career, if someone received a promotion or an award, I *knew* it was political. "Only people who put on dog-and-pony shows get anything in this company," I told people. "You've got to play the game here if you want to get anywhere."

Every year, the company for which I worked gave a Manager-of-the-Year Award, and *every year* I thought I was going to get it. But, every year the award went to someone else. Every year I was very motivated until the announcement was made, and then, when the award didn't come my way, like clockwork, I put out my resume and talked trash about the company.

One year it was announced that there were going to be *five* manager-of-the-year awards along with *five brand-new cars* for top performers. I was excited! I had had a very good year. *I knew I had to be one of the top five,* so I picked out the color I wanted for my brand-new car and anxiously waited for the conference. When the annual conference rolled around … it wasn't me … again. And to add insult to injury, one of the managers who won was a guy named Don Dungy who had been with the company for only one year! Boy, was I mad. I just knew he hadn't earned the award like I had but instead was a schemer who knew how to work the system. I told other managers he was a "good ole boy" who knew how to schmooze with the bosses and as soon as I found a better job, I was outta there!

"Do you really want to know why you didn't get it?"

Soon afterward, my district manager Jeff showed up in my unit and began asking me questions about my negative attitude. I was embarrassed to tell him why I was really mad, but I finally decided it was important that he knew exactly how he had let me down. I boldly asked him, "Why didn't you get the award for me, Jeff?" He could feel my anger and I felt entitled to every ounce of it. "You could have made sure that I got the award, but you didn't … (I wanted to add, *you creep*)!"

In my wildest dreams, I could not have predicted what happened next. Jeff hesitated, then looked me in the eye and said, "Do you really want to know why you didn't get it?"

"Of course I do! I mean, what good reason could there possibly be?"

"Well," Jeff continued, "Pam, I don't think you realize this, but …" Jeff squirmed, cleared his throat and acted like he was preparing to stand before a firing squad, then said, "Well, Pam, in the company, you, uh, have a reputation."

"A reputation? For what? For being the customer service guru? For having the lowest turnover in the company? For generating the most positive comment cards? What reputation are you talking about, Jeff?" I stormed.

"Well, Pam, in the company, you are perceived as a whiner/complainer and that's why you were not considered for manager of the year."

"You've got to be kidding! Me? That's just wrong! I am NOT a whiner/complainer!" Then, I proceeded to whine and complain for another twenty minutes.

"Have you ever heard of tact?"

Jeff eventually stopped my ranting and said, "See! The way you're acting right now is why you have the reputation you do, Pam. Frankly, I didn't try to get the award for you because working with you is difficult! I dread coming to your unit because you don't make me feel successful. You make me feel frustrated. Every time I ask you for something, you have objections …"

"Can't I express my opinions? I didn't know I was supposed to salute! I thought we were encouraged to think for ourselves!" I argued.

Jeff continued, "And, when we have district meetings, you're always the one who has something negative to say about new projects …"

I interrupted again, "I'm just the only one with the courage to speak up, Jeff! Everyone else feels the same way I do. They just don't take the risk that comes with speaking up. Are you going to punish me for being bold and honest?" I knew I had him on this one.

Jeff hesitated. "Pam, I'm not going to argue. Maybe it's just the way you say things. Of course the company wants you to be honest and bold. But, have you ever heard of tact? Why don't you treat corporate the way you treat your associates … or your customers?"

"Because corporate is all screwed up!" I said and that was the end of that conversation. I had told him, and all that remained was to retype my resume and find a company who would appreciate my outstanding leadership attributes.

What are my choices?

Surprisingly, I couldn't find a company that was any more enamored with me than my current company (imagine that!), so I sucked it up and stayed. And then, the unimaginable happened: Don Dungy received a promotion. Guess who my new boss was?

Don Dungy! UGH! I still remember our first meeting. I was like, *whatever.* But Don wouldn't let me get away with that attitude. He stopped our meeting in the middle and gave me two choices: 1) Get on his team or 2) Go to work for someone else!

Gulp! Since I didn't really have another option at the moment, I did some quick calculating and changed my tone a bit. He said he knew I wanted the manager-of-the-year award and if I got on his team, he could help me get it.

Yeah, right, I thought. I'd heard that before. But right away I found that Don's offer was different. Don knew what was holding me back from achieving my goals and he had a development plan for me. He gave me three simple things to do in order to change my reputation in the company. Even though I didn't think the company had it right, I had to admit that perception was reality and if I wanted to get anywhere, I had to embrace his plan and change how I was perceived.

Don did what a leader would do. He helped me change the negative perception so that I could reach my goals. Unbelievably, six months later, I *did* receive the manager-of-the-year award *and* my blue Mercedes. (And by the way, I later understood that Don Dungy was much smarter than I had originally believed. He is now president of that organization.)

You probably have associates who are jealous and bitter. The effective way to deal with those associates does not involve limiting the recognition to your outstanding associates but rather telling them the truth about their standing in the company. Take it a step further and give them an improvement plan. You take a risk with being totally honest, but inevitably you get better results for your risks.

Your associates want recognition. Sometimes they're not receiving recognition simply because they haven't earned it. Other times, they're not getting recognition because they don't know what's holding them back. So they've given up on getting it or, worse, *created inaccurate stories in their minds about why they don't get recognition.* They play the political card because they don't know how else to explain what seems to them to be a system that is very unfair.

Your job is to eliminate the confusion about this "system" so that they, too, will receive recognition. Take this case into consideration: An engineer recently got a promotion and was now responsible for several other engineers, one of whom was more experienced than he and had expected to be the one promoted. The reason why she had been overlooked was performance related, but she had assumed it was a decision partially based on her gender. She was bitter. He asked me what he would have to do in order to move forward in this precarious situation.

I asked him, "Do *you* know the *real* explanation for management's decision to overlook the female engineer and make you the boss instead?"

"Well, yes," he said with some discomfort. "She has this nervous giggle."

"What? Wait a minute. She didn't get the promotion because of a little nervous giggle? That seems a bit odd," I said.

"I know. But you have to understand. We're project managers with very high-profile clients. I've seen it happen in a boardroom; we'll be having a very serious discussion when she'll become nervous or irritated and then inappropriately respond by giggling. I know it's just her way of coping with the tension, but it makes her look incompetent. She isn't, but upper-management couldn't take the risk of our clients *perceiving* her to be incompetent. She'll never get the promotion as long as she does the giggle thing," he responded.

"Well, I guess you have to tell her that," I said.

"What?" He exclaimed. "I can't say something like that to her!"

"Let me get this straight. If you don't explain the giggle thing to her and help her fix this problem, she'll be stuck forever in her current role, right?"

"Yes. That's pretty much the case," he said.

"So," I asked, "if you were her, which message would you rather hear—that you were permanently *stuck*, or that you needed to monitor a nervous giggle in professional environments? In order to adequately perform your role as her manager, you must tell her exactly what prevents her from receiving the recognition of a promotion, regardless of how difficult that message will be to deliver. That's how you move forward in your new role."

Some of you are dealing with similar problems. So before you start dishing out praise to your associates, you will multiply the positive effect of that praise if you will first take those negative, bitter people aside and tell them that you want to be able to reward them and that you want to brainstorm with them about what is holding them back. Give them a development plan so that they can be recognized, and then go ahead and let the praise and recognition flow to whoever has earned it. If you do this, you will feed your environment with energy and enthusiasm!

First, They Must Trust You

But keep this in mind: When you're a new manager, while you may recognize your associates and thank them for their hard work, they will not be motivated by your praise until they know that you can be trusted. They must know that you are not manipulating them just to get what you want!

Once, I was in a situation as a new manager trying to implement a new unpopular company program. The program was set up like this: If we met the new program objectives, the manager would receive a very large bonus. I was very motivated to reach the objectives but no one else really cared … until I promised to share my bonus check with them. When they understood clearly that they would benefit as well from meeting the objectives, they hopped on board. Consequently, the most fun I ever had in my restaurant career was passing out my bonus money after we exceeded the company's new program objectives.

You don't have to give away all your money or bribe your associates, but you must be willing to do whatever it takes to demonstrate your sincere interest in their needs.

Use the Rewarding Performers Checklist to help you get better results from your recognition programs.

✓ Rewarding Performers Checklist

1. Do you believe recognition is important to people?	Yes	No
2. Do your associates feel significant and secure at work?	Yes	No
3. Are you being a "vendor of hope" by noticing their contributions and demonstrating confidence in them?	Yes	No
4. Do you know what motivates your associates?	Yes	No
5. Have you asked your associates the important question?	Yes	No
6. Are you proactive in dealing with jealous and bitter associates?	Yes	No
7. Have you helped your associates identify what is keeping them from getting the recognition they desire?	Yes	No
8. Have you earned the trust of your associates?	Yes	No

Only when your associates know you are truly interested in helping them get what they need will they be interested in helping you get what you need. When they know this, you will be able to effectively use step three in the Essential Plan.

Lesson 6:
Coaching for Better Performance

Keep Short Tabs

Have you ever been in an establishment where someone asked you if you wanted to start a tab? Have you ever said "Yes" to this innocent question? If you have, you may have experienced sticker shock when you finally saw your bill!

If you had opted instead for the *pay-as-you-go* method, you most likely would have avoided this painful experience. You could have decided you were not going to run a tab at all, or that you were going to keep very short tabs. Then there would have been no surprises.

Sticker shock happens at work as well; things build up, seemingly benign problems escalate into huge ordeals, molehills turn into mountains. That is why successful leaders will *keep short tabs* with their associates. As soon as an issue arises, a smart leader will take immediate action to coach associates as needed.

I once learned a great coaching lesson from an associate named Ginger. She walked into my restaurant one day, filled out an application and requested an interview. I was overstaffed at the time and had no intention of hiring her, but her professional appearance and demeanor impressed me so much that I hired her anyway. What had influenced my decision was the current challenge I was having with the appearance of my wait staff. My uniform cost was sky-high yet my waiters were coming to work looking disheveled and unprofessional. I needed to make some changes but was struggling with how to do it. When I saw Ginger's crisp-and-clean appearance, I thought, "This is it. I'll just hire new servers who have higher standards of professionalism. That will take care of my problem!"

I was so proud of Ginger. During the orientation, I praised her for her high standards and asked her to be careful to maintain her uniform just the way it looked on that first day. She gladly agreed and expressed an enthusiastic commitment to my request. And for the first ten days or so of her employment I was pleased to see someone upholding my standards. After that, however, Ginger's attention to detail started to fade a bit. At the end of one month, her uniform looked like everyone else's!

One day, Ginger showed up at work looking as if her uniform had been retrieved from her trunk, buried underneath the tire tools. I was furious. I blew up when she walked in the door and I let her know that I was very disappointed in her. I thought she would be very humble, admit she had failed me, and make a commitment to get back on track. Instead, she said, "This is how everyone else dresses and you never say anything to them. Why are you suddenly picking on me?"

This was definite *sticker shock!* I had *run up a long tab* with Ginger. Neither she nor I knew what the other one was thinking. I had some backtracking to do. It wasn't Ginger's fault that she wasn't meeting my uniform expectations; it was mine. I had failed to follow up with her and with the entire staff, I had failed to inspect daily for uniform compliance and I had failed to provide ongoing coaching to maintain compliance with the restaurant's uniform standards.

From that day forward, I changed the way I dealt with performance issues. I apologized to Ginger for two things: 1) for not talking to her immediately when I noticed a change in her behavior, and 2) for not holding the other servers accountable to the same standard to which I was holding her. I immediately scheduled an associate meeting where we discussed the uniform problem, brainstormed solutions, clarified new guidelines, set a deadline for the new uniform guidelines and agreed on accountability. All that was left for me to do was follow up and make sure I didn't start a tab with anyone by letting things go.

What a relief! The plan worked and uniform standards were back where I wanted them to be. I didn't have to nag or go home frustrated.

I thought I had discovered some cutting-edge management strategy, but in reality, *this was the heart of management!*

Coaching Is the Heart of Management

"Most people would sooner die than think; in fact they do so."

— *Bertrand Russell*

"Real communications happen when people feel safe."

— *Ken Blanchard*

"No life is wasted who has lightened the load of another."

— *Charles Dickens*

"Shall we make a new rule of life from tonight: always try to be a little kinder than is necessary?"

— *James Matthew Barrie, author of Peter Pan*

The word *manager* actually comes from the Latin word *mano*, which means "hand." To manage literally means *to handle*. If you are being paid to be a manager, you are being paid to handle things as they come up. You are being paid to keep very short tabs; to take care of things with ongoing, daily coaching. Managers have to hold themselves accountable for improving their associates' performances every day. If you are going to have a great team, you must take daily coaching seriously. You cannot put off coaching, as many managers do, until the annual performance review comes around. That is not managing.

Can you imagine a successful football coach taking this *wait-until-the-performance-review* approach with his team? He would observe his team on the field, watch them practice but not say a word to the team members. If he saw a team member performing below his capabilities or a player making a mistake, he would just let it go because it wasn't time for the annual review. He would keep his opinions to himself until that designated time.

Not! This would be professional suicide for a coach! Good coaches know that their team has to be ready for the next game. They know there is no time to spare.

But as absurd as this wait-until-the-performance-review scenario may sound, it is often how some managers are handling, or rather *not handling*, their teams at work. Managers walk by non-performers all the time without doing anything. "It's uncomfortable enough bringing up an issue in the review," they think. "Why torture people at other times as well?"

Actually, if coaching is done right, it can be painless and will also make performance reviews painless. Performance reviews do not have to be, and are not meant to be, the only time that honest discussion is shared about performance issues. In fact, this is not the place to bring up anything for the first time. There should never be surprises in the performance review. Performance reviews should only serve as the *formal, documented record* of performance coaching.

This is the positive approach to behavior modification. If you want good results, you have to coach. So what does a good coach look like? When I ask people to describe an excellent coach they have had in their lives, these are the words I hear: caring, committed, motivating, encouraging, passionate about my success, a good example, honest, devoted, and willing to do whatever it takes to help me reach my goals. When your associates perceive you to be their coach, they won't resent your input. They might *resist* at times, because growth can be difficult, but overall, they will appreciate your help. Just remember to address the issue in private and:

Talk openly and honestly about the issues

Don't beat around the bush. Don't be sarcastic. Don't drop hints. Be honest and direct. Say what it is you are concerned about. "I've noticed that you have been late three times this month." Or "I'm concerned about your inability to maintain the uniform standard that we agreed upon."

Meryl Runion, in her book *PowerPhrases!*, teaches managers to "say what you mean and mean what you say without being mean when you say it." This is so important for coaches! If you do not have a copy of this book you might consider adding it to your resource library. Her suggestions have helped countless managers say the important things and avoid saying things that will be detrimental.

Brainstorm solutions

This is the non-confrontational approach to getting the results you need. Asking someone to participate with you in a brainstorming session is much more pleasant than telling them to get with the program. Try asking like this: "Can we brainstorm some possible solutions together?" Or "I was wondering if you and I could talk about things for a moment and brainstorm ways to fix this problem."

Decide on new guidelines

After discussing the issues, decide *together* what will have to be done to fix the problem. If you can't get them to suggest a viable alternative, you may have to direct the conversation. But keep in mind that buy-in will be better if the associate verbalizes what changes need to be made without your prompting.

Set a deadline for new behavior

Decide together when old behavior can be reasonably expected to be replaced by the new, desired behavior.

Agree on accountability

This is the most important step in this model. Make it very clear what will happen if the new behavior falters. If you're careful about this step, the next step will be a piece of cake! Otherwise, you'll have an ongoing problem and more difficult conversations to initiate. By speaking very honestly and saying something like this: "If, thirty days from now, we're having another conversation about this issue, I will have no choice but to start the formal disciplinary process," you'll make it easier on everyone. By agreeing on accountability you will transfer ownership for better performance to the associate. If disciplinary action has to be taken, you won't be the bad guy. It will be crystal clear who is to blame.

Follow up

Always go out of your way to let your associates know that you noticed their improvements. Touch base with them to help them with additional behavior modifications if necessary. And follow through with disciplinary action if necessary. Remember, if you don't inspect for new behavior, your associate will think you have forgotten or that it's not important.

When You Can't Pinpoint the Problem

"Something feels 'creepy' … I just can't figure out what it is … "

Before we close this chapter and go on to the next step in the Essential Plan, I want to mention another major problem related to coaching. Sometimes we feel the need to say something to an associate but don't know exactly what to say without opening a can of worms or turning things into a major ordeal, so we refrain from saying anything. At times, there is a sense that something is just not right, or that an associate is not as open or as enthusiastic as they have been in the past, but we simply can't pinpoint the problem. So we do nothing and things continue from mediocre to bad to worse. How would a good coach handle situations like these?

As in any relationship, the most important thing is to keep the communication lines completely clear. We cannot tolerate any barrier that would impair communications with our associates. Here are some ideas for icebreakers when you are not sure what the issues are:

- "I don't know exactly what's going on or if there's anything I can do to help, but I just wondered if you needed to talk about anything."

- "I don't know if you've noticed, but something seems to have changed in our relationship. Would you mind if we chatted about it?"

- "I can't exactly pinpoint an issue, but I was wondering if we might talk about how you're experiencing your job. Is there something I could do to be a better coach for you?"

- "Would you mind if we talked for a moment? Something doesn't seem quite right and I was wondering if we might brainstorm some solutions together."

Don't let any potential problem build up. You'll either pay now or pay later, and paying later is always more expensive! Use the Coaching Checklist to help you identify areas that may need improvement.

Coaching Checklist

1. Are you keeping "short tabs" with your associates?		Yes	No
2. Is coaching a major priority for you and are you coaching daily?		Yes	No
3. Do you "say what you mean and mean what you say without being mean when you say it"?		Yes	No
4. Do you use brainstorming to avoid being confrontational with associates?		Yes	No
5. Do you hold people accountable for performance improvements?		Yes	No
6. Do you follow up to make sure performance expectations are consistently met?		Yes	No
7. Do you use the disciplinary process when merited?		Yes	No
8. Do you keep communication lines clear even when the issues are cloudy?		Yes	No

Only when you are coaching regularly can you comfortably move on to step four in the Essential Plan.

Lesson 7:
Not Tolerating
Poor
Performance

Top 8 Reasons We Tolerate Poor Performers

None of us wants to tolerate poor performance, but sometimes we feel as if our hands are tied, don't we? We feel as if we have not been given a choice in the matter, or as if we have legitimate reasons for letting poor performers torment us day and night. Here are some of the most common reasons that we believe we don't have a choice and what to do to remedy the situation.

1. We can't let them go because we need them too badly. We are already short-staffed as it is.

This is a common scenario. In every management seminar that I have ever taught, this excuse is brought up by someone. And believe me, I used this one as well.

CASE IN POINT

I had Mario. Mario held my kitchen together. He was a key associate in an upscale restaurant I managed and I couldn't *imagine* life without him. When Mario was there, he accomplished as much as two or three regular cooks and I never had to worry about the food coming out of the kitchen wrong. He was amazing. The only problem was that Mario was mean. In fact, his nickname was Gorilla! He would storm into work, never talk to anyone, work like a machine and then leave.

Some of the biggest problems I had with Mario occurred when a waiter would make a mistake on an order and have to ask Mario for help. This would make Mario mad, so the associates would have to ask for the assistance of one of the managers. It was a hassle and I didn't like dealing with things in this manner. I knew this fear of Mario's wrath was bad and was negatively affecting the morale of the entire restaurant. But what could I do? I needed Mario. We all needed Mario. So, we tolerated Mario ... until I went on vacation. One night in the middle of my peaceful vacation, I received a call from my assistant manager David.

"Pam, I hate to tell you this, but we had to fire Mario."

"What?" I screamed. "You're kidding me, aren't you? What could Mario have *possibly* done to get fired?"

"Well, Pam," winced David, "Carol and he were arguing over one of her orders, and she called him Gorilla to his face and, well, he came over the line and punched her."

I have to admit that my first response wasn't, "Is Carol OK?" but rather "You had to fire him for that?" I was so convinced that I couldn't make it without Mario that I was willing to tolerate just about anything from him. I had lowered my standard so much for Mario that he could almost get away with murder! Luckily, Carol was not injured in the ordeal, but my can't-make-it-without-Mario plan was!

And here is the amazing part of this story: We made it without Mario! In fact, after the initial shock and short adjustment period, things were actually much better without him. The other cooks were so relieved he was gone, they gladly worked a little harder to fill in the gap that his absence left. The morale went up among the waiters as well, and I spent less of my time and energy putting out the fires caused by Mario's bad temper.

I had allowed myself to be held captive by my misconception that I couldn't make it without Mario. Consequently, *I* wasn't running my restaurant. Mario was.

I wish this was an isolated case, but I know that this scenario is being played out in countless arenas all over the world. We, as conscientious leaders, must not be duped into believing that someone who is not on our team is indispensable to our team.

2. They are close to retirement

One of my client companies recently asked me to do an analysis of their administrative staff. They were having some morale problems and needed help getting to the bottom of things. After I had interviewed the associates, it was obvious to me that the problem was with one particular associate. This associate, Martha, had been with the company for many years. Her knowledge of the company rivaled that of the owner and the chief officers, but she was so incredibly bitter that no one wanted to deal with her. When someone in the office needed to ask Martha a question or receive minor assistance from her, she made the co-worker feel as if he or she were requesting one of her kidneys. No one enjoyed working with Martha. She had been counseled numerous times with no improvement.

When I shared my findings with the owner of the company, I made the recommendation that they continue the disciplinary process and let Martha go. The owner quickly objected and said that would be impossible. When I asked why, he said, "We can't let her go, she's about to retire. Let's just let it happen naturally. That would be easier on everyone."

Unfortunately, she had been going to retire for five years! The staff continued to be tormented by her and the productivity continued to be adversely affected by her attitude.

If this is your situation you may want to consider these factors:

1. Everyone, including Martha, is suffering in this situation. It is not a kind way of dealing with people to allow them to stay in a situation where they are miserable or have low job satisfaction.

2. Martha wants to leave the company in an honorable manner; therefore, this is leverage to get improved performance from her. Start or continue the disciplinary process in order to let Martha know that she does not have the option of staying in her current position unless she changes her demeanor. A good leader cannot and will not tolerate low performance from any team member, even if it is the most tenured associate.

3. They may file a lawsuit or an unemployment claim against us

While serving as the chief operating officer of a company, I found myself using this excuse when the owner asked why I wasn't proceeding with disciplinary action against a certain associate. The owner, Walker Harman, sometimes referred to as "Hardball Harman" because of his master negotiation skills, immediately called me on this. I'll never forget the lesson he taught me.

Walker did not want a lawsuit or unemployment suit any more than I did, yet he knew that when our company made decisions based on fear, we were consequently putting ourselves in a position of disadvantage. He encouraged me to "get my ducks in a row"; make sure I followed procedures, documented everything and did everything possible to "save" the offending associate. After that I could move ahead with confidence. If an associate sued our company, then I had nothing to fear. We had acted in good faith and had not been paralyzed with fear. He assured me that the price of an occasional lawsuit was less than the price of compromising our company's values by not doing what we knew needed to be done.

4. They have a desperate family situation

This may be the most common excuse that I hear from managers. "If I fire that associate, his life will fall apart!" or "You don't understand how terrible her situation is!"

Formerly, I would allow myself to be tortured by these thoughts as well. I would lose sleep, toss and turn all night long, feel like a jerk and then resolve to let the under-performer stay … *until* I totally grasped this: Associates are responsible for themselves. I am not responsible for terminating them; they are responsible for allowing themselves to be terminated. By allowing under-performers to remain employed, I'm not helping them; I'm hurting them. I'm allowing them to make excuses for themselves. By doing this, I am enabling them to stay on a path that will be ultimately more destructive than the path of being terminated.

5. I inherited the problem associates

When I used this excuse with my boss, she accepted it … *at first*. Then one day she looked at me and said, "I'll accept that excuse for ninety days only. After that, those associates are your problem."

She was smart to push me to accept responsibility for my own success. She knew that ninety days would give me the time necessary to either replace those associates or get them on my team. If getting them on my team meant I would have to retrain or spend time coaching or start disciplinary action, then I would have to prioritize my time and energy to do so. But I was not helpless. I did not have to tolerate poor performance. She definitely was not going to tolerate poor performance from me!

6. HR won't let me fire them

This situation is similar. The associate is perceived to be "protected." Usually, HR has its reasons for not allowing you to proceed in the way that you are inclined to proceed. In that case, you may try saying to your HR representative:

> "It would be very beneficial for me to hear your understanding of the situation with _____. At your convenience, would you be willing to spend some time discussing her case?" or "I feel frustrated by this situation. What can I do to gain your support in dealing with this associate? Is there any way that you can assist me so that this situation will improve?"

It is crucial that you go out of your way to demonstrate to HR your cooperation and respect. If they perceive you to be on their team, you will earn their confidence.

7. They work for a labor union or for the government

In almost every seminar that I lead, I hear this excuse. Not long ago, I led a class in which the majority of the attendees were either union or government employees. When I began to discuss termination, several people spoke up and said, "You don't understand. What you're teaching sounds good, but it won't work here. You can't discipline or terminate people where we work!"

"Really?" I said, trying to think quickly on my feet. I was scrambling to find an answer to this dilemma since I had never worked in that type of environment. But, before I had the time to respond, a man sitting on the front row spoke up with authority and said, "That's not true. I work for the union and for the state. You can discipline and you can fire, it just takes longer."

I asked him to explain.

"I'm an engineer for the state and was promoted to lead a group of civil engineers who were formerly my peers. One of the first tasks of my new position was to do formal performance appraisals. As I began the process, I realized I had to make a choice: Give honest reviews or the merely perfunctory reviews the engineers had been accustomed to receiving. Because I was going to be held accountable for their performance and knew that each of them had been performing below their capabilities, I made the difficult decision to be honest and thorough in the appraisals. As a result, every one of the engineers filed grievances against me with the union. For three months my life was miserable, going through hearings, dealing with the dirty looks and the icy stares from my former friends and working in the unstable environment produced by that lack of trust. Sometimes I wished I had never been promoted, but I stayed with it. I knew I had done the right thing and I knew I had the documentation to back up what I had written on the reviews."

"Well, what happened?" I asked.

"The rulings came out in my favor. One of the engineers quit, but the others are still there, performing at a much higher level." He hesitated for a moment and then added, "And, as a result of my management of this situation and others like it, I've been promoted to the role of chief engineer for the state."

He went on to encourage the other managers in the class to work within the system to get the results they needed. He said, "The system is set up to prevent discrimination and unfair treatment, not to prevent you from getting optimum performance. The system may make the discipline process longer, but if you're not afraid to use the system and have the tenacity to work through the process, you'll get results."

8. They're related to the boss

There are many variations of this common problem. And whatever variety of "special relationship" to the boss you are dealing with, it's always a sticky problem! But you're not helpless here. If you present your case in a mature manner, you'll be surprised at what you can accomplish.

In most cases, your boss wants the company to be profitable and productive. Your job is merely to show your boss how the effect of tolerating low performance from that particular associate is costing money or productivity, is negatively contributing to the poor health of the company and/or is endangering your boss's future success.

It will never do any good to go whining to your boss about an associate in whom that boss has some type of personal investment. They will not believe you. They have psychological reasons for not wanting to believe you. Unless you show them the hard, cold facts, they will NEVER believe you or have a reason to stand behind you.

But if you have done everything in your power to transform that person into a productive associate and you're still not getting the results you desire, take these steps:

1. Keep a record of the time you're forced to invest in this associate or in fixing problems precipitated by this associate.

2. Show your boss the "opportunity cost" (how you could have been spending your time) and what that translates to in dollars for the company.

3. Ask your boss to brainstorm solutions with you for resolving the situation.

In order to resolve a problem like this, you have to be able to speak to your boss's greatest need. You have to speak their language. You must ask yourself, what drives my boss?

Remember, *address the need of the listener* (Chapter 4). Whatever it is, that is what will get their attention.

We, as human beings, will never make any change unless we perceive that change to be one that will help us either avoid more pain or experience more pleasure. Somehow, your boss is associating pleasure with keeping that associate in place or pain with the thought of letting that associate go. As negotiators, we have to help them associate more pain with their staying or more pleasure with their dismissal. For instance, if what drives your boss is the perception that they are helping this special associate and they must make that investment in them by keeping them employed, no matter what the cost, then your job is to demonstrate how your boss is not helping that associate by leaving them in the position.

There Are Fates Worse Than Firing— Don't Lose Sleep Over It

Just a word to you about the sleepless nights you might experience worrying about terminating a low performer. Remember, if an associate has to be terminated, that associate has chosen to be terminated. They fired themselves! You can quit beating yourself up for being a mean boss. You are not the culprit in this case.

It is also important to remember that being fired is not the worst thing that can happen to a person. Sure, no one wants to feel like a loser and no one wants to have to go out looking for another job. But no one wants to be stuck in a job where things aren't working either. There are fates worse than being fired. One of those fates is being in a *dead-end relationship*. If someone is in a job where things aren't working for them, for whatever reason, that is a serious dead-end relationship.

Fire With Class!

And finally, a word of warning: Sometimes it is legitimate guilt that is troubling you about a termination. Maybe you lost your temper. Maybe you failed to follow proper procedures. Maybe you didn't offer the associate enough help. If any of these is the case, go back; do it right; take care of business, then continue the process. But please, please, please, don't just let it go!

✔ Do Not Tolerate Poor Performance Checklist

1. Do you often feel as if your hands are tied?	Yes	No
2. Do you feel as if someone is keeping you from getting the results you need?	Yes	No
3. Are you often frustrated at work?	Yes	No
4. Are you willing to do whatever it takes to get the results you need?	Yes	No
5. Do you use your power of appeal with your boss?	Yes	No
6. Do you let associates stay because no one wants to endure the discomfort of the disciplinary process?	Yes	No
7. Are you convinced that you help everyone involved when you refuse to tolerate poor performance?	Yes	No
8. Are you convinced that you will punish everyone involved if you tolerate poor performance?	Yes	No
9. Do you fire with class?	Yes	No

Your power as a manager is in holding to the Essential Plan. Many managers give up and accept a situation even though it is a compromise to do so. A true leader will not do this. A true leader will recognize this as a *management pitfall*.

Lesson 8:
Avoiding Management Pitfalls

It's Harder Than It Looks

Managing people is like raising children: *Everyone* knows how until they have some! It was so easy to criticize former bosses when they failed to act in the most mature or insightful manner, wasn't it? "If I were the boss, I would treat my people more fairly" or "I wouldn't be so mean" or "I'd give my associates what they wanted!" But now that you're in the role, you find yourself saying and doing the same things you hated when other bosses said or did them to you! What happened?

Help! I'm becoming my worst boss!

Maybe you failed to take into consideration the *new pressures* that come with the job of managing. As with raising children, before you are a parent you think that it should be easy to say a simple "No," and you wonder why parents don't take better control of their offspring. Then, when you have a son or daughter (and he or she steals your heart away), suddenly you're being manipulated and find yourself struggling with the simple "No"!

You failed to take into consideration the *new emotional pressures* that come with being a parent. But, how could you have known? You were totally unaware of that dimension until you passed into that new realm.

Bingo! This is the exact problem you face as a new manager. Prior to your promotion, you were unaware of the pressures your bosses had from above—the pressure to adapt to company criteria, the pressure to meet the performance expectations of their boss, the pressure to keep their jobs! Add to that the emotional pressure that comes with juggling the expectations of associates, customers and personal life. This produces a seriously high-pressure environment for anyone. No wonder you're struggling with your new role.

What Are Management Pitfalls?

Management pitfalls are behavioral patterns that you've learned by default. They come naturally. You get stuck in these behaviors because you don't really know what else to do. You never move forward when you get stuck like this. That's the definition of insanity: Doing the same thing over and over again and expecting a different result.

Management pitfall #1: Roll your eyes

You don't even have to be in an associate's presence to use this technique. You just have to think about them. Automatically your eyes roll up. You sigh and mumble to yourself something like, "I work among morons," "I can't believe that" or "Why me, God?"

You are stunned by the way people act. You are insulted or maybe totally frustrated. You are the boss, but these associates make you feel like being the boss is not an honor but rather some kind of absurd punishment! Rolling your eyes is your response. You think rolling your eyes is a management prerogative.

But, does it accomplish anything? It may help you feel better for a few moments or it may help you justify your own frustration, but it won't ever get you results. In fact, if your employees see you rolling your eyes, it could possibly affect your credibility. When you are viewed as baffled, defenseless or helpless, you're seen as more vulnerable and it becomes easier for others to take advantage of you.

Being a student of human nature will keep you from falling victim to this particular pitfall. Your frustration will be minimal if you understand what makes people do what they do.

Management pitfall #2: Complain

Complain to your boss. Complain to your peers. Complain to other associates. Complain to your family. Complain to your dog or cat. Complain to everyone *except* to that associate. You can't help it. You've got to vent. You've got to let it out. An associate is driving you crazy and you talk about them all the time.

When I was a brand-spankin'-new assistant manager in my first restaurant, Thelma was a key employee who had worked there for eighteen years. Thelma made my life miserable and *everyone* knew about it. When I was at a managers' meeting, I was always complaining about Thelma. Thelma was the topic when I was on the phone with my girlfriend. Thelma was the topic of our dinner conversations at home with my husband and small children. I talked about Thelma so often that my kids felt like Thelma was part of our family. My son Hudson is now twenty-six. I saw him the other day and he said to me, "Mom, how's Thelma?"

What? Clarifying moment: I know it's sad, but I had inadvertently made my problems with Thelma an indelible part of Hudson's childhood!

We think complaining makes us feel better. One thing is certain; it doesn't make anyone else feel better. And it certainly doesn't help Thelma.

Management pitfall #3: Avoid the associate

You dread going to work. You try to get your schedules adjusted so you don't have to work with those bothersome associates. You ask for a transfer or try to get them transferred. You walk the other way when you see them. But you can't escape their presence or the trouble they cause you. If only they weren't there, then your job would be tolerable.

Avoidance will only prolong your agony—or someone else's agony if you allow them to transfer to another location. Meeting the situation head-on, talking honestly with the associate, brainstorming viable solutions with them and holding them accountable to performance standards will get you the results you need.

Management pitfall #4: Fume

It simply eats at you. It burns inside you like a smoldering campfire. Every new offense fuels the fire of disgust that you feel toward the associate's actions. You are inches away from "going postal." But, you hang in there, spend more of your profits on antidepressants and antacids and dream about revenge.

Managers who live like this make everyone in their lives miserable. Eventually they burn out or simply lose the respect of their followers. But there is one thing fuming does accomplish; it serves as a warning that *you* are not doing your job. At the very first sign of anger, STOP and ask yourself these questions:

1. Have I set clear expectations for the behavior I desire?

2. Have I been fair and consistent in rewarding desired behavior?

3. Have I had honest coaching sessions to direct desired behavior?

4. Have I held associates accountable for desired behavior?

If the answer is "no" to any of these questions, you've lost control of the situation. You may think that you don't have the power to change what's happening to you and you feel like a victim. But the truth is, you never have to be a victim. Your hands are not tied behind your back. Even in the worst-case scenario, when you haven't been given the power to discipline an associate, you still have the power to speak honestly to your boss and solicit help. If, for some reason, that help is denied, you can always look for another job. But, *it is never a rational option to stay in a situation that is driving you crazy.* If you visited with a psychiatrist about this problem, you would be told to either 1) remove the situation that is causing your anger or 2) remove yourself from the situation. There are no other options!

Management pitfall #5: Fire in a rage

You fire someone in a rage, in the heat of the moment, after the last straw falls onto the stack. Someone pushes you into a corner and you come out fighting. It seems like the right thing to do at the moment, like you don't have a choice. And, boy, does it ever feel good to say, "YOU'RE FIRED!"

But the weeks and months that follow are a different story, especially if your boss is not convinced. You lose the support of your boss (if you ever had it to begin with). You lose your credibility with the staff. They didn't have to be there to see what you did. Within twenty-four hours they all hear some version of what happened: "Did you hear what psycho-boss did?" Oops! You established the wrong precedent. By your actions you said to the associates, "I am either unpredictable or out of control." And, to top it all off, you may even face legal ramifications.

Management pitfall #6: Punish passively

But perhaps you don't have the power to fire someone (even though you would love to) or maybe you work in a system that makes it very difficult to let someone go. Or maybe you are simply uncomfortable with the Essential Plan. Consequently, you feel stuck in a terribly frustrating position. You feel helpless, that you are doomed to spend the rest of your career with this set of mediocre associates that someone else hired. So you come up with other, passive means to get what you want. Your reasoning goes like this, "If I make their lives miserable, maybe they'll quit." So you give them the bad shifts or fewer hours without talking to them about it first. You take away their overtime or give them overtime. You hope they'll get the hint. They should know better than to act the way they do. They are *so* going to suffer for it. You just alter the schedule, run and hide, and allow other managers to deal with their questions.

This is the "chicken" way of dealing with poor performance. Besides being ineffective, it is an unkind way of dealing with people. But it happens all the time. Managers are uncomfortable saying the hard stuff so they do this instead.

A kind, gentle woman who was a director of a home-hospice nursing organization once admitted to me that she used this method. She said she gave the most difficult patients to the nurses with whom she wasn't happy. This was serious punishment, not just for the nurses but for the families of the seriously ill patients. And she looked so sweet and harmless!

Now, there is absolutely nothing wrong with using the schedule as leverage with associates. What's wrong with it is *not talking to them first* and letting them know why you do what you do. The schedule is a great way of giving positive or negative reinforcement, but you will not get the full impact from using this tool unless you explain what you are doing *before you do it*. Then it is not only effective, it is also fair and considerate.

Management pitfall #7: Hope they quit

Changing the schedule didn't work and it doesn't look like there's going to be any help from your boss or human resources, so you secretly hope (and maybe pray) they quit. You don't talk about it, but this is what you do.

You hope they quit because you feel trapped. You feel the associate is non-productive and your workplace would be better off without them. Unfortunately, this is a very common experience in management. So many times, poor performers have been allowed to stay on the job and everyone suffers as a result. In most environments where I have consulted, I have found this rule to apply to all employees:

20%	60%	20%
All there	Half there	Shouldn't be there

In general, twenty percent of the associates employed in an organization are star performers; they're fully connected and fully engaged. The next sixty percent are associates who are only partially connected and partially engaged. The bottom twenty percent are sometimes referred to as "flat-liners" and probably should have been terminated long before you met them. For whatever reason, they haven't been and you're stuck.

But if you ever catch yourself hoping someone will quit, let it set off an alarm in your brain. You're not managing. You are abdicating your responsibility as a leader. *You* are now being managed by your situation. The 20-60-20 rule applies only in environments where leadership is conspicuously absent. And even if you're not the primary decision-maker in your workplace, you still have the power of appeal (see chapter 7). If you decide not to use that power, you'll be stuck indefinitely.

I hope you haven't already succumbed to one or more of these management pitfalls, but if you have, quickly change whatever you're doing and get out! If you don't, you're in danger of arriving at the next stop: The *management "recycle bin."*

Lesson 9:
Managing Yourself

The Ten Management Commandments

Statistics show that approximately one third of all managers either will burn out due to the drain of dealing improperly with associate challenges or will be "thrown out" into the management recycle bin due to avoidable fatal errors involving ethics and/or simple management etiquette.

If you want to avoid being in this statistical category, you need to know and practice the *Ten Management Commandments:*

1. Never lose your temper

> *"You are the master of the spoken word but a slave to the words that should have remained unspoken!"*
>
> — *Abraham Lincoln*

It is totally normal to experience frustration in your job. You will have those days when you are angry with your associates, with your boss or with your own performance, but if you allow others to see you lose control, *you will lose credibility.* Of course, sometimes calculated anger serves a purpose in management, but losing your temper *does not demonstrate calculated anger.* If you lose your temper at work you are saying this to your associates: "I am out of control." And, if they think you are out of control they know that *they are now in control!* You have just given your associates an excuse to ignore you because they see you as unreasonable, immature or irresponsible. Whatever it takes, you need to develop control over your emotions before you walk into your work environment.

Drive-time is a great place to clear your head, expect the best and *get prepared for the worst.*

2. Never gossip

> *"Small minds talk about people; Average minds talk about events; Great minds talk about ideas!"*
>
> — *Anonymous*

Even if an associate is your friend, never discuss sensitive information that has the potential to harm or mislead. This is one area where you can distinguish yourself as a leader quickly. Mature leaders are aware of the harmful nature of *all gossip* and will always seek to turn conversations toward something productive and positive.

Many managers are most tempted when it comes to bad-mouthing their predecessors or others who may be viewed as a challenge to their own success. Associates may pull you into this type of conversation. But when an associate wants to share negative comments about another manager, a true leader will always redirect the conversation: "I understand your frustration with your circumstances, but what can I do to help you now?" If someone will talk behind the back of your enemy, they will also talk behind your back.

3. Never speak negatively about your boss to anyone in your organization

> *"You can tell more about a person by what he says about others than you can by what others say about him."*
>
> — *Leo Aikman, Writer and Newspaper Editor*

Regardless of how frustrated you may become, this is political suicide. Some managers think they will earn points for the "valuable insights" they have which, they think, will make them look more capable than their superior. But in reality, the opposite is true. Your boss needs you to be on his team, and when you demonstrate that you're not on your boss's team, you've said, "I'm not a team player" or "I'm interested only in my own advancement, regardless of who I have to walk over to get there." I know it's frustrating to work for a boss who seems to be incompetent, but there is a way to deal professionally with this situation and *it is not bad-mouthing them to their bosses, your peers or your associates.*

If you have something to say about your boss's performance, you must say it to your boss. If that doesn't work, you must ask permission to go over your boss's head. If you don't, prepare for a rocky road ahead and prepare to be a sitting duck if you are ever lucky enough to get their job!

Whatever you say about your boss, someone will also say about you. You reap what you sow!

4. Always listen more than you talk

"The greatest good you can do for another is not just to share your riches, but to reveal to him his own."

— *Benjamin Disraeli*

This one is really hard for some bosses to do. When I was a regional supervisor, my CEO once called me into his office and asked me to change my vocabulary. He said that I was spending too much time telling people what to do!

I was confused. "Aren't bosses supposed to tell people what to do?" I asked.

"Yes," he said, "but if your associates feel as if it *was their idea* they will be more prone to do what you are asking." He then encouraged me to say "What do you think we should do?" instead of simply telling associates what to do.

5. Always take complete responsibility for the tasks you are assigned and the mistakes you make

"Do not blame others for your failure to be fully accountable for your own life. If others are to blame then you have given them control!"

— Bob Perks

When I trained managers in the restaurant industry, I always began the training with this statement: "You will be ahead of ninety-eight percent of all your peers in management if you will simply *do it* now! It is so easy to postpone difficult tasks and to make excuses for poor execution. Managers who do not postpone but, instead, *hold themselves accountable* will move up quickly. The more difficult the task, the more aggressive you should be in pursuit of completing that task."

I still believe this is one of the most important "management commandments." Make sure you're keeping a "to-do" list, working your list and preventing any assigned task from falling through the cracks. If your list is too long, you may need to delegate or enlist the help of subordinates, but never over-promise and under-deliver!

In addition, when things are going poorly, don't blame someone else. When you do this, be aware; your bosses will see this tactic as evidence of immaturity and a lack of leadership, because your bosses are not measuring you by the mistakes you make, but rather by how you accept complete responsibility for mistakes and recover from them.

It is imperative that you believe this *and model this behavior for your associates.* Make it a point to tell associates in the orientation, "There is no mistake you will make in your job that I have not already made myself. So please don't be afraid to admit mistakes or ask for help." As it does for you, this approach will take a weight off their shoulders, help relieve undue anxiety and set an associate up for success!

6. Never foster unrealistic expectations concerning salary increases or promotions

$$E1 \div E2 = S$$
(Experience ÷ Expectation = Degree of satisfaction)

This formula shows the powerful effect of our expectation on our experiences. If our experience is good, but our expectation is unusually high, our degree of satisfaction will be very low. I'm not saying that you shouldn't expect the best. I am saying that if *you expect too much too fast, you may be disappointed.*

In the management ranks, if you haven't already noticed, there has never been a shortage of big talkers. Anyone can talk the talk. Not many successfully *walk the walk.* If your boss is insightful, she will not be hasty in judgment. It takes time to tell the difference between a *good talker* and a *good walker!* She will know that the proof of your words is in your consistent performance over a period of time. Any supervisor who's been around the block has seen her share of flash-in-the-pan performances. You must be patient as your trustworthiness is proven. Being ambitious is good. Being unrealistic has the potential to destroy your career.

Early in my career, this was a major challenge for me. I was constantly in a state of discontent because things were not happening fast enough for me. If you're experiencing frustration due to this challenge, keep this formula in mind when assessing your situation at work. Things may be better than you think, but if you have unrealistic expectations, you won't realize how good they actually are until it's too late.

This formula applies in everyday life as well. So often, unrealistic expectations derail the best of relationships. A mature individual will monitor their expectations and respond maturely when dreams are postponed.

7. Always show respect for your associates

"Really big people are, above everything else, courteous, considerate and generous—not just to some people in some circumstances— but to everyone all the time."

— Thomas J. Watson

Showing respect starts with how you think about your associates. Authentic concern for their success, for their careers and for their general well-being will help you avoid disrespectful behaviors.

Sounds easy! But frequently, you're forced to deal with people who don't demonstrate respect for you. If this is the case, please don't give up. There are proven tactics that you can use to gain respect from even the most stubborn or obnoxious associates. Just don't get into a situation where you are acting as immature as they might be. Remember the story I told about Thelma? If you don't have a Thelma now, you may in the future. So let's talk about how to handle all the male and female "Thelmas" of the world.

CASE IN POINT

When I was first introduced to Thelma, I was very kind and enthusiastic, and told her how much I was looking forward to working with her. Her response to me was, in a very dry tone, "You're number thirty-seven. I've worked for thirty-six managers before you, Missy, and I can already tell, you won't last very long."

I was stunned. "What? Why do you think I won't last long? Why would you say that to me?" I said, trying to hide my discomfort.

"Because you are very naïve," was her immediate retort.

"No, I'm not," I said quickly.

Yes, I was. And, now I realize I could have vastly improved my management experience at that restaurant by simply saying this in reply: "You know what, Thelma, you're probably right. I probably am naïve and I'd appreciate it very much if you would point it out to me if you overhear me say anything naïve or see me do anything naïve. Will you do that for me, Thelma?"

To say that to her would have taken a whole lot more humility than I had at the time. I had too little confidence in myself to give Thelma that gift. But had I used this tactic, I would have saved myself so many sleepless nights and agonizing drives home, stressing over tattle-telling Thelma. If I had made her my "teacher" and taken on the role of her "student," she would have been more likely to join my team, because then she could have taken some credit for my success. Since I didn't do that, her mission was to get me fired.

A woman managing a remote group of international associates resonated with this make-them-the-teacher tactic. She related how she was leading a *team* of "Thelmas" from Japan. She said they were all very polite to her and always said they would do what she asked, but promptly disregarded her requests. When she challenged their uncooperative behavior, the associates would use the language-barrier excuse. The manager said none of her tactics were working *until* she enrolled in a Japanese class. Afterwards, when she had demonstrated interest in their language and allowed them to help her learn, the barriers began to fall away. Her Japanese has improved somewhat and the improved productivity of her team is off the charts!

In general, people will not trust you until they know that you really care about them. It is not enough to tell them you care; you will have to prove you care.

8. Always care more about the success of the people who work for you than about your own success

"A good manager is a man who isn't worried about his own career but rather the careers of those who work for him. My advice: Don't worry about yourself. Take care of those who work for you, and you'll float to greatness on their achievements."

— *H.S.M. Burns*

In a recent seminar, a manager responsible for information technology at a prestigious school confided his fear about training people to his level. He admitted that the young technology graduates hired by his company knew more about current technology than he did. This caused him anxiety. He said, "It's only a matter of time before I lose my position to one of these trainees, so I don't teach them everything I know about the school. If I did, I might work myself out of this position. I have to be careful. Do you think I'm doing the right thing?"

"Yes, if you want to sabotage your own career!" I said.

A manager is being *paid* to work himself out of a job. If you are building competent, successful replacements for yourself, you are *more valuable* to your organization! That's the quality of real leadership most lacking in the world. Don't *ever* worry about one of your trainees out-shining you. Help them succeed and you will help yourself succeed. *(Refer to Appendix B, the "Triple A" Club.)*

And if by chance you are working for someone who doesn't recognize this quality, don't worry. There are hundreds of companies out there who do. Just stay committed to helping others succeed, because the more committed you are to the success of those around you, the brighter your future will be!

9. Never resent the success of a peer

"The one important thing I have learned over the years is the difference between taking one's work seriously and taking one's self seriously. The first is imperative and the second is disastrous."

— Margaret Fontey

Frequently, you will be in direct competition with a peer who will seem to receive more honor or respect than you. This is always a supreme test of character. At this point, it's easy to be tempted to undermine their work, take potshots or refuse to assist this associate. If you take this tactic, you will only hurt yourself and establish a reputation for not being a team player. If you remember to think *more about getting results* and *less about getting credit,* you will find success in unexpected places.

Also, in reference to unhealthy peer competition, *never, never, never discuss your salary* with someone in your organization other than your boss. This is not acceptable even if a co-worker initiates the conversation and seems to want to discuss it in a very benign manner. This conversation will not benefit you or them in the long run. This is basic management etiquette.

You will demonstrate class and maturity when you follow this rule and resist unhealthy competition.

10. Never be a victim or play the role of martyr

> *"The diaper we wear in childhood represents the first and only time in our lives where we get exactly what we want just by hollering for it. From the minute we take them off, we have to figure out other ways of getting people to do what we ask of them."*
>
> — *Harvey MacKay*

I hope an alarm will go off in your head if and when you ever feel you cannot get the results you need from other people. This book and other management resources clearly teach that we have power over our futures. You have the power of appeal, you have the power of your own passion and you have the power of the universe behind you when you are working for the common good.

Often the thing that makes the difference between a mediocre manager and one who is outstanding is simple tenacity to do whatever it takes to get the job done regardless of the obstacles.

If you are representing yourself to your supervisor as a victim, be aware: Your boss may read this as a lack of true leadership. Your boss is looking for someone who will take charge, see what needs to be done and take the initiative to do whatever the job demands.

Remembering these "Ten Management Commandments" will be essential to your success and your happiness in a management career. Take time to think about these often, especially the ones that you don't think are important! You will need to practice all of them in order to thrive.

Lesson 10:
Training Your Brain to Stay Changed

Choosing

So, how do I stay on track? Good question! Many managers *plan* to change or improve but fail to sustain significant change or improvement. How will you be different? How will you follow through with your good intentions and the desire you have *today* to excel in your role as a leader?

We all know that consistent focus on your objectives will give you consistent results. Only by consistently following the Essential Plan and obeying the "Ten Management Commandments" will you consistently avoid the management recycle bin and stay away from management pitfalls. But *knowing what you should do* and *actually doing it* are two different things.

> *"One can choose to go back toward safety or forward toward growth. Growth must be chosen again and again; fear must be overcome again and again."*
>
> — *Abraham Maslow*

In this quote, Maslow pinpoints the key to staying on track; it is in *choosing* again and again and again and again. It is in *choosing* to move forward every day. It is in *choosing* to feed your brain with words and images that will encourage you to make the right choices.

Successful leaders choose to read inspiring books from other leaders. Successful leaders choose to listen to CDs on their way to work. Successful leaders spend time listening to and watching role models or mentors. Successful leaders choose to program their subconscious mind to make the right choices. *Successful leaders choose not to leave their future to chance.*

If you are serious about being the leader the world needs, you will have to choose to spend time every day focusing on your plan of action and focusing on your goals.

Oops! I Blew It! What Do I Do Now?

So, what if things don't go as planned? What if you really blow it? If that happens or has already happened, it is *never too late* to go back, admit your mistakes and start over. Start over every day if you have to. You will be respected for doing this. What will get you in trouble is acting like there is no problem or no need to backtrack.

Forgive yourself!

Many managers (including me) have spent way too much time beating themselves up for past mistakes. We allow ourselves to be tormented by "I should have said … ," "Why didn't I do this instead of that" and so on. When we finally get to the place that we can own our humanity and forgive ourselves for not being perfect, our lives at work will improve.

If you remember that even your role models and the best leaders have seriously blown it at times, you may go easier on yourself. And when you become more generous with yourself, it will help you become more generous with others as well.

We are all struggling to get by in this world, to be who we are meant to be. My personal pep talk for being more generous with myself and with others goes like this: Don't take yourself so seriously. We *all* have our "stuff." We are *all* in various stages of mental illness. *We are all learning as we go!*

Remember, You Are a "People" Too

When you are struggling to regain your patience, or to find a way to motivate or inspire a stubborn associate, it may benefit you to remember that we all share the same flesh and blood. It is important to remember that you are a "people" too. We all share the same needs, fears and desires. We all need significance and security. We all need hope.

One day while working, I felt very discouraged. I felt as if my efforts and hard work were going unnoticed and unappreciated. I had zero energy to perform my job and was thinking seriously about quitting. As I walked through my restaurant, I noticed similar signs of discouragement on the faces of my associates, and it dawned on me; they're experiencing the same thing I am! Oh, my! I've failed to notice them. I've failed to appreciate them. I've failed to give my associates the hope I'm feeling the lack of right now.

From that day forward, I was more aware of our shared humanity and it became easier for me to understand what was going on with my associates and how I could better support and encourage them. This was an *essential* revelation in my management career.

In conclusion, I hope that this book will provide you the essential support and the essential revelations you will need on your management journey. I hope you will refer back to these chapters for advice and for encouragement. And I hope you will implement the techniques and strategies of the *Essential Plan*.

If you do, you are guaranteed success. And the success you achieve will be an essential part of the success of countless others.

Good luck in your journey as you become an exceptional leader and as you multiply the effect of your leadership in a world that desperately needs leadership. I hope to hear about your success!

Appendix A

What's Your Bore Score?

This brief test will help you determine how interesting you are in your workplace interactions.

To answer each question, enter the value representing the degree to which it describes you:

0 Never   **1** Hardly ever   **2** Sometimes   **3** Frequently   **4** Always

After you have read the questions and graded yourself honestly on each one, total your scores and find your rating on the chart on the next page.

(If you want to verify your rating, let your boss or an associate answer these questions about you. Then compare the scores.)

1. Do you repeat gossip?

2. Do you tell your associates things that irritate you about other people?

3. Do you find it boring to listen to other people's stories?

4. Do you talk to your associates about your aches and pains?

5. Do you think about what you are going to say while someone else is talking to you?

6. Do you feel like you never have anything to say to your associates?

7. Do you dread going to work?

8. Do you think about the bad things that could happen to you at work?

9. Do you think that the world is a dangerous place and one can't be careful enough?

| | 10. Do you look forward to being at work because it gives you the opportunity to tell your associates about everything that is going on in your life? |

| | 11. Do you think that life is boring? |

| | 12. Do you think that life is disappointing? |

| | 13. Do you wish that outgoing people would just "button it up"? |

| | 14. Do you think your ideas are better than everyone else's ideas? |

| | 15. Do your associates look at their watches or yawn when you are talking to them? |

| | 16. Do you look at your watch or yawn when your associates are talking to you? |

| | 17. Do you feel there are not many interesting people in the world? |

| | 18. Do you choose carefully whom you will have a conversation with? |

Calculating your bore score

Total number of points: _____

Your Bore Score:

0 – 18   You are probably a very interesting person!

19 – 36   You may want to refer to the Triple-A Club discussion in Appendix B

37 – 54   You may be a total bore

55 – 72   You may be the cause of global boring

Appendix B

The "Triple A" Club

Which side are you on?

Anxious	Aware
Angry	Appreciative
Arrogant	Available

As a manager, you have a tremendous effect on your environment and on the culture of the workplace. Every manager is in the "Triple A" Club. Some are on one side and some are on the other. If you are on the *good side* of the "Triple A" Club, you are consistently **aware** of everyone in your environment: Who they are, what they are experiencing, their level of happiness or sadness, etc. You will also be consistently **appreciative**; you will notice the efforts people make, the contributions they bring, the uniqueness of each individual and the innate value of everyone you encounter. You will also be **available** as a source of hope and support to people around whom you live and work. You will always be asking, "Is there anything I can do for that person?" instead of feeling helpless to make a difference.

Being on the other side of the "club" will keep you from being aware, appreciative, and available. On the *bad side*, you will spend your days **anxious** about protecting your own career, anxious about what others think and say about you, anxious about your own performance. You may also be **angry**: Angry at your boss, angry with your organization or angry about circumstances in your life. On the bad side, you will also be **arrogant**. You may have grown accustomed to being a jerk in order to get your way—using intimidation as a management tool—or you may simply display the "whatever" variety of arrogance because you have lost interest in the people with whom you work.

Which side are you on?

Appendix C

Essential Quotes

"I learned this, at least, by my experiment; that if one advances confidently in the direction of his dreams, and endeavors to live the life which he has imagined; he will meet with a success unexpected in common hours." — Henry David Thoreau

"Most people never run far enough on their first wind to find out if they've got a second. Give your dreams all you've got and you'll be amazed at the energy that comes out of you." — William James

"When you get into a tight place and everything goes against you, never give up then, for that is just the time that the tide will turn." — Harriet Beecher Stowe

"My greatest point is my persistence. I never give up in a match. However down I am, I fight until the last ball. My list of matches shows that I have turned a great many so-called irretrievable defeats into victories." — Bjorn Borg

"In the middle of difficulty lies opportunity." — Albert Einstein

"We can never really be prepared for that which is wholly new. We have to adjust ourselves, and every radical adjustment is a crisis in self-esteem: we undergo a test, we have to prove ourselves. It takes inordinate self-confidence to face change without inner trembling." — Eric Hoffer

"The world is a great mirror. It reflects back to you what you are. If you are loving, if you are friendly, if you are helpful, the world will prove loving and friendly and helpful to you. The world is what you are." — Thomas Dreier

"Let no one come to you without leaving better." — Mother Teresa

"The lives of great men all remind us we can make our lives sublime and, departing, leave behind us footprints on the sands of time." — Henry Wadsworth Longfellow